INSIDE

We could fill a whole book with Clash Royale top moments. From the moment you install it and play your first game, to the oohing and aahing as you first win a Magical Chest, and the wailing out loud as your tower crumbles in the dying seconds of overtime. Clash Royale is just jam-packed with memorable moments. Here's our top 20 best ones...

Remember your first

Crown Chests are nice and Gold Chests aren't bad, but they're not nearly as generous as a Giant Chest. The first time you're awarded one of these big old boxes you'll uncover more gold than you can shake a goblin at, as well as somewhere between eight and 30 rare cards, depending on your arena level. You'll never look at one of those piddly Silver Chests the same way again.

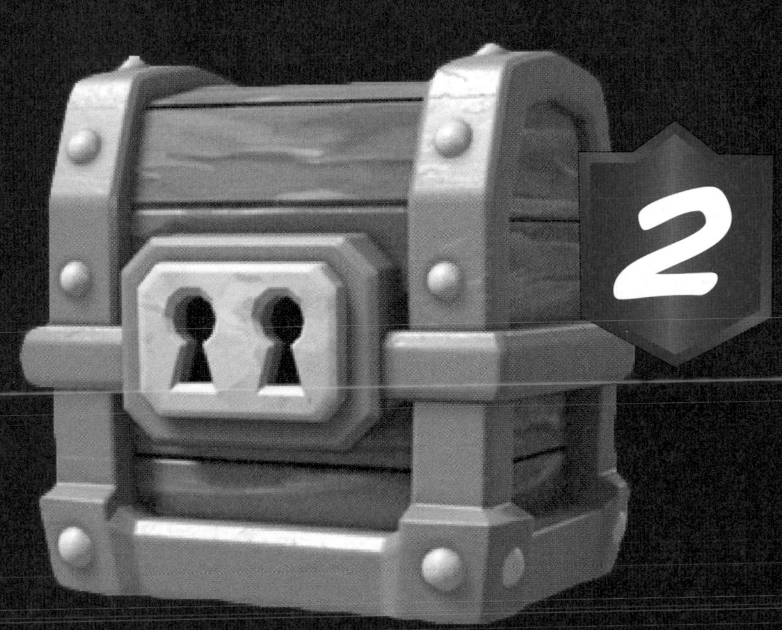

Let battle commence

Although Clash Royale has been available for quite some time in certain parts of the world and to certain lucky players, its global launch was 2 March 2016. This was the date when Clashers from all over the world were able to log on and get scrapping, in a worldwide celebration of card-based battling. And it's only got better since then...

3

Gloat simulator

There's nothing quite like the excitement of a closely-fought round of Clash Royale, and it's always a thrill to earn a narrow win against a worthy opponent. Victory tastes even sweeter when you have the chance to gloat, though, so tap on the crying king emote for a satisfying opportunity to make your vanquished foe absolutely furious.

Moving on up

A win in Clash Royale is always a pleasure, but it's extra-exciting when those congratulatory trophies take you over the threshold to unlock a brand new arena. The opportunity to do battle in a new arena isn't just a visual change, either - each new battleground you unlock will add rare and powerful cards to your chests, too!

Spark of genius

Clash Royale was great in May but it became even better in June, when Supercell launched its biggest update to the game yet. The developer made chests more generous and improved the Card Shop, but the most exciting change was the addition of six brand new cards, including the Fire Spirits and Guards as well as legendaries such as Sparky and the Miner.

Driven to distraction

Distracting high-damage troops away from your Crown Towers is a handy tactic in Clash Royale, and a great way of keeping your foes in the firing line of your tower archers for longer. Done right, you can completely neutralise some of your adversary's scariest cards, drawing a Mini P.E.K.K.A. away from an unguarded tower, for example, with nothing more than some cheap Goblins.

The best of the best

Clash Royale's first ever tournament took place in January 2016, when eight of the most tactically-talented YouTubers gathered to compete for arena dominance. After a hard-fought campaign, it was Chief Pat that emerged the victor, making his mark as Clash Royale's first champion of champions.

I am legend

The rarest cards in Clash Royale are incredibly hard to come by, and you could play for months without finding a Lava Hound or Miner in your Crown Chests. But that only makes the moment you uncover your first legendary card more memorable, and you're sure to look back fondly on the time you found a fearsome Ice Wizard or plucky Princess in the middle of a chest-opening sesh.

From the jaws of defeat

We've all played rounds of Clash Royale that have got off to a bad start. Perhaps the enemy surprised you by rushing down an unguarded lane, or perhaps your concentration wandered from the match for a moment. But determination is a virtue in the arena, and the pleasure of losing two crown towers, only to bounce back and snatch victory from the jaws of defeat, just can't be matched.

The one musketeer

The Musketeer doesn't just look cool - she's also a long-range sharpshooter. And perhaps the most satisfying way to make use of her gift for marksmanship is by taking down an enemy Cannon. These great big guns can be a real pest, but they have a fairly short range, meaning your plucky Musketeer can simply shoot them to bits from a distance without taking a single hit.

11

Clan you dig it?

Clash Royale's clan system isn't just a way to exchange tips and chatter with a friendly community of Clashers - it's also a great way to get your hands on the cards you need most. So, if you're not finding any Musketeers in your chests, you can always ask you comrades for a donation, and there's nothing better than logging on to find you've received a hefty gift from one of your kindly clanmates.

Hog wild

The Hog Rider is a fearsome card, and perhaps one of the strongest offensive units in the game. Let this rider approach your opponent's Crown Tower before dropping a Freeze spell to halt all enemy resistance, and then simply sit back and watch as he tears that tower apart. Throw some Goblins into the mix too for even more damage - and even more satisfaction.

13

Enter the dragon

When you first start playing Clash Royale, the Baby Dragon can seem horribly overpowered. It's got decent health, can fly above your melee units' attacks, and it deals splash damage to wipe out your hordes of low-health troops. That's why it's such a great moment when you realise you can take out a Baby Dragon with a single well-placed Archer card, distracting the flying lizard from your tower before it can even deal damage.

Team Rocket

Not only is the Rocket the most powerful spell in the game in terms of raw damage, it's also a pleasure to watch as it sputters its way across the arena before landing in an intense little fireball. That pleasure soars to new levels when you're using the Rocket to finish off an enemy Crown Tower, of course, smashing through their defences with an unavoidable missile.

14

15

Mad as a box of goblins

Watching a barrel filled with daredevil goblins fly across the arena is always guaranteed to raise a smile, but a perfect launch is extra special. Perhaps you've got a giant soaking up damage, the enemy has just depleted their elixir reserves with a mistimed spell, and then - BAM! Their crown tower is covered with goblins. It's a joy to behold.

16

Throw in the towel

Sometimes it can be clear that you're going to win the match, but you just can't break through to your opponent's final Crown Tower. Sure, it's a victory, but you'll only receive two crowns for all your hard work, leaving you with more to do if you're working towards a precious Crown Chest. That's why it's so appreciated when a losing player simply gives in and lets you steamroll over that final tower.

17

Elixir to spare

Winning a game of Clash Royale usually comes down to a matter of elixir advantage. Maybe you've made good trades throughout the game, or perhaps your opponent fluffed a few spells, but whatever the reason it's always a pleasure to enter the final moments of the game with enough currency to utterly overwhelm your enemy.

No ifs, ands, or huts

Spawner decks are some of the most frustrating foes to face in the Clash Royale, and it's often difficult to know how to counter a player that simply fills the arena with hut cards. Fireballs and Poison are both handy, but that moment when your perfectly-timed Rocket hits three huts and a Crown Tower? Priceless.

18

19

Bundle of bones

The Skeleton Army can be a pretty scary card, summoning a swarm of skellies that can take down your toughest tanks - or even your precious crown towers - in the blink of an eye. As such, it's always supremely satisfying to drop a perfectly-timed Arrows card on this eerie army, turning a fearsome threat into a harmless bundle of bones.

20

What's mine is yours

Elixir Collector decks can be infuriating to play against, since they'll often start slow but end the game with an enormous and untouchable elixir advantage. That's where the Miner comes in, tunnelling below all of your enemy's defences to get right to their collectors, and tearing them down before your annoying adversary can even respond.

CLASH OF CLANS

ESSENTIAL STRATEGY GUIDE

There's so much to get to grips with in Clash of Clans, that if you're a complete newbie, or a seasoned fighter, you need our six page strategy guide!

Clash of Clans is a global game of base-building strategy and tactical attacking that takes place in a colourful world of beefy Barbarians, fearsome Dragons, and spooky skeletal warriors. But just because it's vibrant doesn't mean that it's easy, and you'll have to use all your wits and cunning if you want your village to thrive.

The core of the game can be divided into two sections: defending and attacking.The first is a matter of building up your village, placing Cannons and Mortars to bombard attackers as well as constructing sturdy walls to keep invaders away from your precious resources. But when you attack another player the tables are turned, and you'll have to deploy your armies carefully to avoid your opponent's carefully arranged fortifications.

Victory depends on your ability to succeed at both attack and defence, and there's a whole world of players out there who won't make it easy. So read on for our top tips on how to establish yourself as a Chieftain to be reckoned with.

SIMPLE

01

02

Get a headstart

Every player begins Clash of Clans with a special Shield that will prevent all attacks for three days - use this time wisely and you can get a headstart on the competition. Build as many Gold Mines and Elixir Collectors as you can to ensure a steady flow of currency, and make sure you've got an upgraded Gold and Elixir Storage building to stash your cash. Prioritise these, and then rush to lay down some Mortars and Archer Towers before your Shield expires.

Don't be a big spender

At the very start of your Clash of Clans career, you'll be handed a nice little pouch of precious gems as an introductory freebie. It's important to know, however, that gems are in much shorter supply once the game gets going, so it's crucial to spend them wisely. Builder's Huts are by far the best use of gems early on, and you should keep saving up for all five of these before splurging on boosts or resources.

03

04

Don't be hasty

Upgrading your Town Hall is always a treat in Clash of Clans. Because, for each Town Hall level you advance, the building will gain more storage capacity, be more difficult for enemies to take down, and unlock an array of exciting new structures too. But, generally speaking, you should upgrade all of your existing defences and units before upgrading your Town Hall, or you'll quickly find yourself outmatched by higher level enemies.

Go it alone

Multiplayer may be the name of the game in Clash of Clans, but Supercell has thoughtfully included a single-player mode to help you get to grips with the basics of attacking an enemy base. There are 50 stages on offer, each offering a sterner test of skill than the last. It's a great place to start developing your strategy, and there's gold and elixir on offer for each base you bash to bits.

INTERMEDIATE

Know your shield

Every time your village is successfully raided by an enemy Chieftain, you'll once again find yourself under the protection of a Shield, and it's important to understand this system in order to maximise its benefit. A Shield protects you from all further attacks for a limited time, but its duration is shortened every time you do a multiplayer attack. You might be better off upgrading your defences and earning resources in single-player while it's active.

Yes we clan!

The clue may be in the name, but an awful lot of Clash players still aren't part of a clan. But there are loads of advantages to joining up with a community of like-minded Chieftains, including the ability to share tips and tricks or even request reinforcements from your comrades. And don't be afraid to switch to another clan if your first choice isn't especially active or friendly - there are plenty out there to choose from, so find one that works for you!

Keep watching the skies

Walls, Cannons, and powerful Mortars are certainly important, but you have to remember that not every attack will take place at ground level. Even relatively early on in the game, you'll have to contend with enemy Balloons dropping bombs all over your carefully-planned base. As such, it's important to make use of the Archer Towers, Air Defenses, and Wizard Towers if you want to stand a chance of repelling these aerial invaders.

Compartmentalise

An enormous circle of double-thick walls protecting your key structures might sound smart on paper, but this kind of village layout proves horribly vulnerable to Wall Breakers in practice. The trouble is that their explosive attacks will simply burst through both layers of wall at once, leaving all that extra defensive potential wasted. That's why it's better to arrange your walls to form many smaller compartments - the enemy will have to blast through them all to get to your most precious buildings.

Expect the unexpected

Whether you're storming the enemy ramparts or building your own fortifications, it's often easy to forget about traps. But, used properly, they can be the difference between a glorious victory and a crushing defeat. When attacking, it's wise to test for traps by sending in one or two weaker troops to check for bombs or spring traps. And as a defender, remember that traps don't require a builder to construct or re-arm. Handy.

Don't overcommit

When you set eyes on a well-defended village, your first instinct might be to throw every Giant, Goblin, and Archer you have onto the battlefield. But while this approach might seem sensible, it can often lead to you expending troops that were never needed in the first place - or sending some of your best soldiers to their doom unnecessarily. Sometimes, it's best to stay calm and assess the situation before committing more troops.

Chicken out sometimes

When you tap that big glowing Attack button, Clash of Clans will automatically try to find you a suitable opponent to trade blows with. Sometimes, though, the game will pit you against a terrifying fortress filled with traps, defences, and impregnable walls. At times like these, it's often best to simply walk away and search for another foe, rather than wasting all your troops on a suicide mission.

Take your revenge...

When you log into Clash of Clans to find your village in ruins, it's time to take revenge. Simply open up your defence log, and you'll see a long list of every brigand and brute that's attacked your village recently. Tap the revenge button and you'll have the opportunity to scout out their defences before deciding whether or not to attack. Alternatively, you can peek at their village, head back home, and then start building the perfect army to take them down...

Use a tailored army

Whether you're bashing bases in the single-player game or taking revenge on old attackers, it's worth spending some time spying on the enemy's defences before launching your assault. Then you can build an army specifically designed to take apart that particular village. So, if they're lacking in air defence, you can build some balloons. If their walls are weak, add some Wall Breakers to your army and explode your way in.

Prioritise your protections

There's never quite enough defensive structures to protect all of your buildings. You might only have enough walls to protect your Town Hall and a few Elixir Storage tanks, for instance, leaving your Collectors and Clan Castle perilously exposed. That's why you have to prioritise. So, if you're trying to hoard gold and elixir, make sure you concentrate your defence on your Storage buildings.

ADVANCED

15

Huddle close

Constructing and upgrading powerful defensive structures is important, but if they're not placed properly these pricey buildings are basically useless. One important principle is to place defences quite close together, so that any enemy troops attacking your Mortar will be exposed to your Cannon fire, for example. Another is to put your most powerful defences close to the centre of your base - otherwise the attacker can pick them off early.

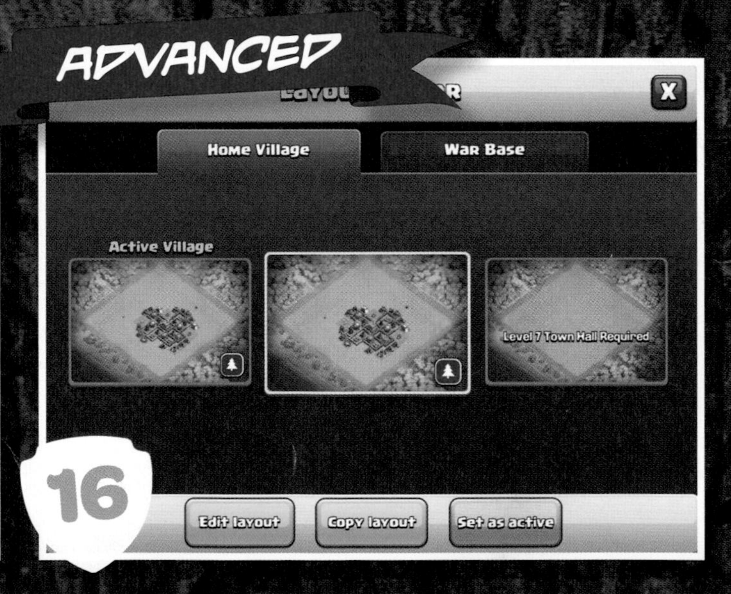

Investigate the editor

Switching between different village layouts can be a fiddly process, especially if you just want to spend a day or two farming for resources before switching back to your more usual arrangement of buildings. That's where the Layout Editor comes in handy, allowing you to save multiple layouts and switch between them whenever you fancy. It's also worth saving screenshots of your favourite creations - or of particularly tough enemy bases.

Choose your targets

By now you'll know that you don't have to attack every village that the multiplayer matchmaking suggests to you. Some might look too strongly defended for your Goblin horde to handle, or perhaps you don't want to throw all of your Balloons and Dragons at a base full of Air Defences. But even if you find a village you think you can conquer, it's important to check that it has enough resources stockpiled for you to earn back what you've spent in troops.

Take the easy wins

Not every win has to be a majestic three-star victory, and sometimes it actually makes more sense to think a little smaller. So, if there's a heavily-fortified village with a couple of Collectors and Storage tanks dotted around its outskirts, it might just be worth dropping a few Goblins or Archers to nab those resources rather than committing to a full-scale assault. You'll walk away richer without taking on any significant risk - that sounds like a victory to us.

Watch those replays

Nobody wants to wallow in defeat, but every loss should be an opportunity for you to improve your village layout and adjust your defences. You should be watching replays of every successful enemy attack and paying close attention to which areas of your base are proving most vulnerable to attack. Is that one wall getting breached every time? Upgrade it! Is there one angle of attack happening over and over? Stick a cannon down there!

Two tribes go to war

Once you've found a Clan you get along with, upgraded your defences, and built up a formidable army, it's time for Clan Wars. The epic three-day events pit your Clan against a rival faction, and give you 48 hours to prepare a War Base that'll make mincemeat of any invaders foolish enough to approach. You can also use this time to scout enemy War Bases, and compose an army to take them down. Then, it's Battle Day. Attack twice and bring glory to your clan!

MISSING PIECES!

Help fill the holes in this battle scene from Clash of Clans!

IT'S WAR! But first you have to make sure all the troops are present and correct. Match the missing pieces to the holes, and then check you're right - the answers are at the bottom of the page.

ANSWERS: A:1 B:4 C:2 D:3

CLASH ROYALE

SUPER HARD CARD QUIZ!

Not all Clash Royale cards are as common as each other. Test your knowledge of nine of the rarer examples in the deck. Answers below – but no peeking!

4

ANSWER: ....

5

ANSWER: ....

6

ANSWER: ....

8

ANSWER: ....

7

ANSWER: ....

9

ANSWER: ....

Answers

1 Dark Prince
2 Golem
3 Guards
4 Ice Wizard
5 Miner
6 Princess
7 Royal Ginat
8 Sparky
9 Three Musketeers

CAN YOU FIND HAMMERMAN?

Help your Heavy navigate his way through the maze to find Lt. Hammerman...

HELP YOUR HEAVY GET TO LT. HAMMERMAN BEFORE IT'S TOO LATE!!!

HOW MANY SKELETONS CAN YOU SPOT?

There are skele-tonnes of them. How many can you spot?

WHY SO GLUM?!

YAY! I DID IT! I COUNTED: SKELETONS

WRITE YOUR ANSWER HERE...

Our bony friends are good for several things in Clash Royale. Like surrounding a Giant and rattling him until he falls over. Kind of a pity they're so easily wiped out by arrows. Here we've amassed a pretty good army, but (including any you can see in buildings), how many skeletons are in this pic?

SUPERCELL

Discover the brains behind your favourite games!

Supercell is the company behind the Clash games, and Boom Beach, as well as the older, but great, Hay Day.

We caught up with the Clash of Clans man, Jonas Collaros, who told us a few secrets about how they make their amazing games and keep them at the top of the charts...

"Clash Of Clans has been an incredible success, and loads of other games try to copy it. What do you think is its secret sauce?"

"Well, I think when people are trying to figure out what's the secret recipe, it's quite often that they look in the wrong places. It's not a numbers thing. I would say a lot of the strength of the Clash Of Clans team comes directly from the Supercell culture as a whole. It's partly about keeping the team really small – the original team was just five or six people, and it's still only 15 people.

Having a small team that's very independent and has passionate developers that play and care about the game is really the secret. It sounds a bit fluffy, but lots of times, when you're deciding what the next features of the game will be, and what our next release is going to look like, you have to have this sense for what feels good. Not only as a game maker, but also as a player.

SUPERCELL

Started: 2010
Country: Finland
Employees: 180
Website: www.supercell.com
Games: Hay Day, Clash Of Clans, Boom Beach, Clash Royale

For me, it's mostly about the fact that we all play the game and care about the game – we're designing it for the players as well, and we want to enjoy the changes that we're making. It's very rare that we spend time in our day's work talking about how to make money and things like that. We're focused on designing the game."

"Has it always been smooth sailing?"

"No, that's pretty much the universal thing – it's never always smooth sailing; there's always something you can be doing better, and there's almost always something that you're doing wrong.

One thing that we've been trying to get better at is making the company more flexible in terms of getting new ideas and games out there.

There's no shortage of ideas for games, but very few of them ever make it to a beta stage. So a lot of talk at the company has been about how we can get faster. How do we find the good ideas faster? How do we kill the bad ideas faster? How do we get people who are interested in the right ideas together at the right times? And how do we manage this with the live games, and the successes that we have at the moment? That's a very difficult challenge, especially for such a small company, and we've been

All of Supercell's games, including the monster that is Clash Of Clans, are built to last, which means ever-evolving feature sets

constantly having to improve.

Our way of working is about making games that will last in the long term, games that we can work on for the long term. I can't see us just throwing out new games as fast as we can just because we can. That's not the sort of long-term approach we want to take."

SPOT THE DIFFERENCE...

AT first glance, they look almost identical scenes, but look closer and you'll start to see some subtle differences. There are actually plenty of differences between the two, but some are fiendishly different. See how many you can spot and write your answer in the space below...

WRITE YOUR ANSWER HERE...

YAY! I DID IT! I COUNTED: ______ THINGS CHANGED

MISSING PIECES!

Can you complete the puzzle by matching the missing pieces?

IT'S a confusing scene, with enough TV screens to give you square eyes! Can you help fill the holes in this missing puzzle by matching the pieces that have fallen out? You can see if you're right by checking the answers below.

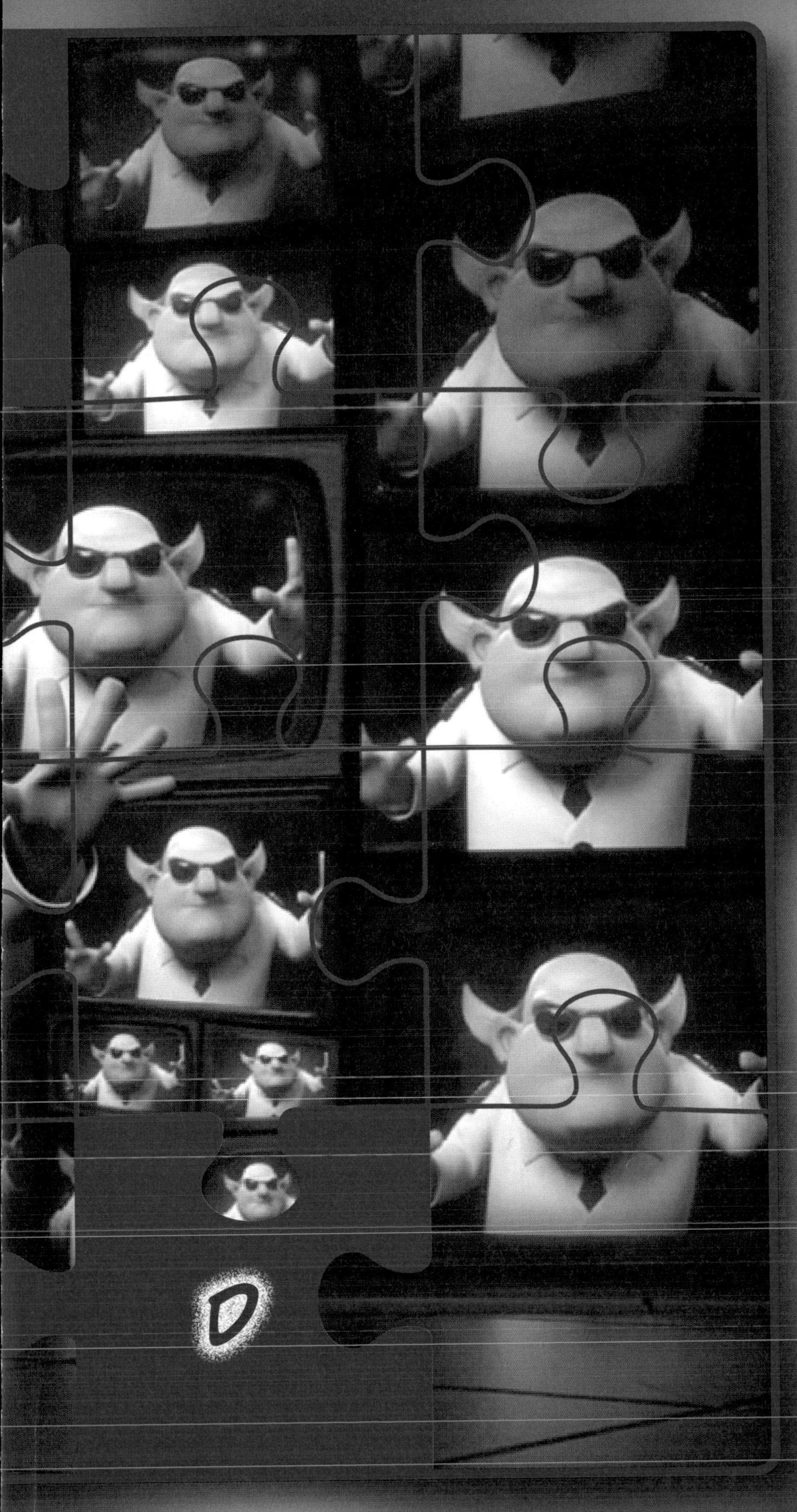

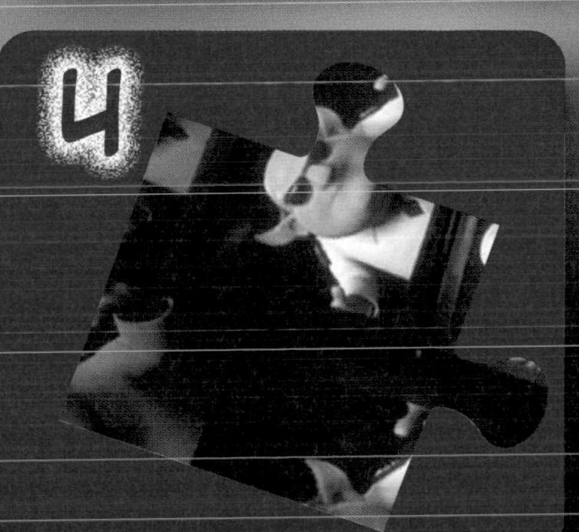

ANSWERS: A:4 B:1 C:3 D:2

CLASH OF CLANS'

TOP 20

MOMENTS

Every game has its moments, but - as any Clash of Clans fan will tell you - high points and low points in Supercell's epic are anything but rare. Whether it's punching the air the first time your clan topples another, or fighting that urge to throw your phone against a wall when your own town gets torn apart, there's rarely a dull moment in Clash of Clans. That's exactly why we've decided to gather up our top picks here, in a handy little rundown.

Launch Day

Do you remember what you were doing on August 2nd, 2012? We'd imagine the boys and girls at Supercell's HQ were pacing around feeling rather nervous, for that's the day Clash of Clans first rolled out on iOS. Four years later, and it's still sat atop of the charts, with millions playing each day. Not bad, eh?

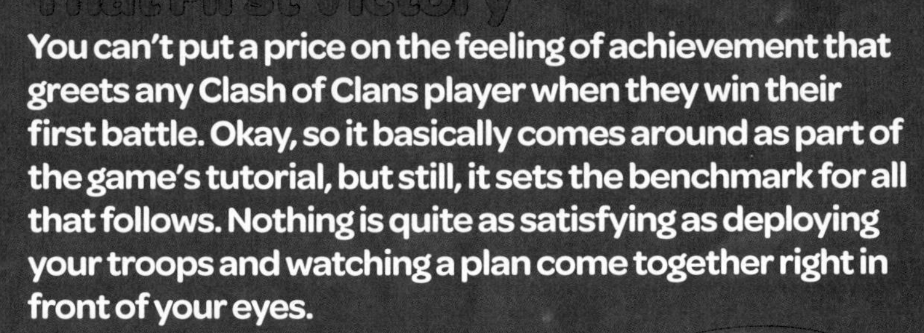

That First Victory

You can't put a price on the feeling of achievement that greets any Clash of Clans player when they win their first battle. Okay, so it basically comes around as part of the game's tutorial, but still, it sets the benchmark for all that follows. Nothing is quite as satisfying as deploying your troops and watching a plan come together right in front of your eyes.

That First Defence

Almost as good as taking out a rival's base is returning to your own to find out your defences hold up when under attack! The design of your base in Clash of Clans is probably the most complex but important part of play, and seeing others flounder as they attempt to smash their way in is about as satisfying as it gets.

The Heroes Update

What's a battle without an immortal hero to back your troops up? Clash of Clans' version 3.3 update - launched all the way back in October 2013 - brought heroes into play for the first time, adding The Barbarian King and The Archer Queen into the game to mix things up. This was also the first time Dark Elixir was brought into play, allowing players to recruit heroes and upgrade their abilities.

ClashCon 2015

Little over three years after Clash of Clans made its debut on the App Store, Supercell's superstar title had amassed enough fans to support the game's very own conference. The very first ClashCon hit Helsinki in October of 2015, and brought with it talks, panels, question and answer sessions with the folks behind the game and, of course, a live tournament.

Feeling Decorative

One of the most popular facets of Clash of Clans is the ability to decorate your base from top to bottom with items from the shop. Flags, statues, flower beds and torches are all available, but they actually serve a purpose, blocking the deployment of enemy troops and, as a result, funneling them towards danger if placed in the right spots. Devious!

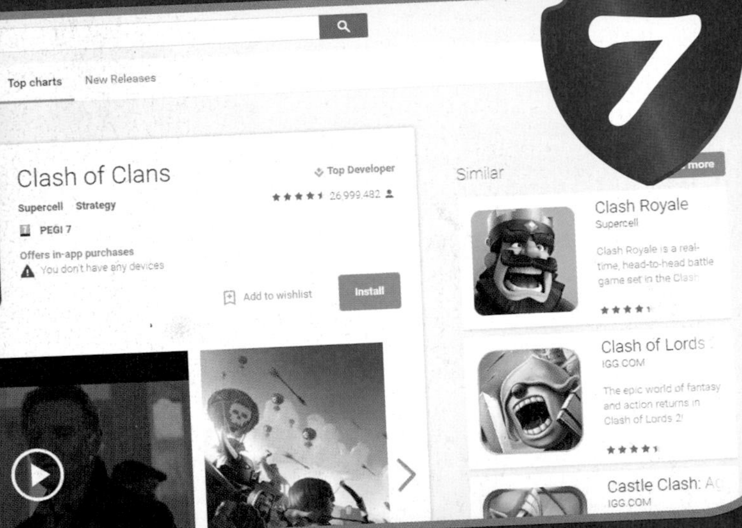

Launch Day, Part Two

Of course, Clash of Clans hasn't only made its mark on iPhone. A year and two months after it rolled out on Apple's platform, Supercell pushed it out on Google's, with Android day one bringing yet more millions into the Clash of Clans fold. Three years on and, as you might expect, Clash of Clans remains the biggest game on Google Play, with Supercell's other efforts - Clash Royale and Boom Beach - not far behind.

Joining A Clan

It may surprise newcomers to learn that it's perfectly possible to play through Clash of Clans quite happily without ever joining a clan, though doing so is of course part of the fun. Doing so doesn't come easy though. First you'll have to rebuild your Castle at a cost of 10,000 gold. Once that's done, you'll be given the option to join or create a Clan.

9

100 Million Daily Players

Just how many people are playing Clash of Clans every day? Officially, we just don't know, although back in March this year we did find out that, if you pool it together with Clash Royale and Boom Beach, more than 100 million people every day are firing up one of Supercell's classics for a battle or two. To put that in some context, that's almost twice the population of England!

10

The Dark Elixir Drill

While you might think your only way to grab yourself some Dark Elixir is to steal it from rival bases, in fact you can also deploy a special drill to dig down into the earth to scoop some up for you, raid free. As with all things in Clash of Clans, however, good things come to those who wait, and dropping in your first drill doesn't actually come until you reach level 8!

11

Clash of Clans Goes 3D

Ever conscious of staying ahead of the curve, last year saw Supercell attempt to give players a new perspective on a Clash of Clans raid, taking the game into 3D. A video uploaded onto YouTube in November 2015 took a typical battle and dropped the camera down, letting players see from a first-person, 3D perspective for the first time.

12

The Delaying Game

One advantage of joining a clan is that it opens up additional troops, courtesy of your clan mates. Now, these troops won't defend your base outright, but there's a certain amount of satisfaction that comes with watching them delay enemy attacks, giving your foe an extra hurdle to clear before they can move onto attacking your base proper.

13

The Town Hall 11 Update

There are piddly little bug fixing updates, and then there are big, bold, brash updates that change everything, like Town Hall 11. Packing in a new hero, new artillery, bigger maps and a whole host of other new or updated features, for many, Town Hall 11 was a bit like pressing the reset button on the whole Clash of Clans experience - this was a whole new world, and one that took some time for even experienced players to master.

14

That Three Star Attack

It's important to note that not all victories in Clash of Clans are equal. While destroying 50 percent of your rival's base is nothing to be sniffed at, you'll only pick up one star for that achievement. Two stars are unlocked if you also take out your enemy's Town Hall, while the ultimate three star accolade only comes about if you destroy everything in sight. Pick up three stars, and you're just a little bit special.

15

The Launch Of Clan Wars

It seems bizarre now, but there was in fact a time when Clash of Clans didn't have any Clan Wars. That update - described by Supercell at the time as the "biggest Clash of Clans update ever" came in April 2014, and it took the world by storm. Now players could pick up bonus loot as clans took each other on, all without losing resources, shields or trophies. Play has never quite been the same since.

16

That First Defeat

It seems odd to celebrate a loss in Clash of Clans, but every defeat - whether seeing your base destroyed or failing to flatten someone elses - brings with it some vital lessons. Did you take the wrong troops into battle? Are your walls laid out in the wrong places? It takes a few losses or more to really illustrate what you're doing right and what you're doing wrong in play. Learn those lessons!

17

The Day Supercell Toppled EA

Less than a year after Clash of Clans hit iPhone, something amazing happened; the small, Finnish developer overcame a giant. Yes, in December 2012, clever people good with numbers worked out that Supercell was making more money from the App Store with just a couple of games than the almighty Electronic Arts was with its entire library. Needless to say, Supercell has stayed on top ever since.

18

Upgrading Your Town Hall

Nothing signifies your progress in Clash of Clans as much as upgrading your town hall from level to level. Not only does this make your base more difficult to take down, but it's also the best way to show rival players you're on the way up. Don't upgrade too early though! Make sure you've upgraded all your troops, walls and buildings to the maximum first.

19

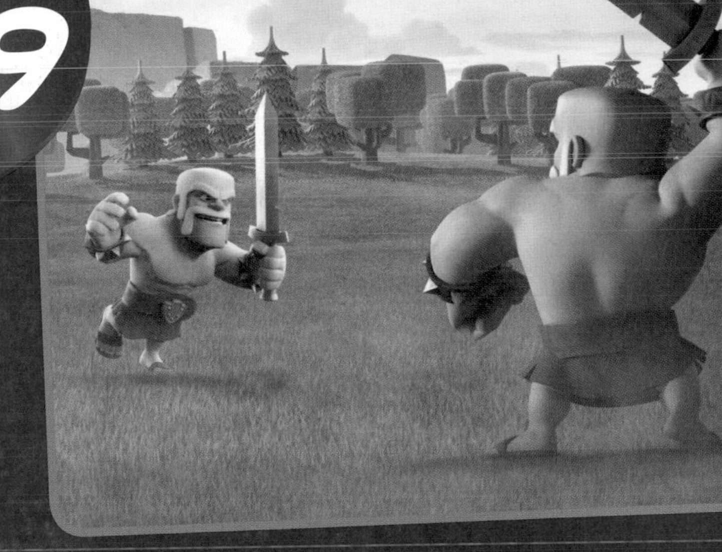

The Balancing Act

Of course, when you have a game with as many players as Clash of Clans that's as updated as often as it is, making sure millions get to grips with the changes and stay on board is a massive exercise. That's why the last major update to play, which rolled out in May 2016, was one big balancing act, keeping the game competitive without making it too unfriendly, too unforgiving for newcomers.

20

Turning The Tide With A Spell

Using a spell in battle really is a moment of magic. It's not an exaggeration to acknowledge that spells, unlocked at level 8, really can turn the tide of a battle. Lightning, Healing, Rage and Jump Spells are all available, and deploying them at the right time really can flip a battle on its head, reviving tired troops or weakening your rival's defences. There's no sweeter victory than one snatched from the jaws of defeat.

CLASH ROYALE

GET MORE FROM YOUR GAME!

It's easy to jump in and play a few quick rounds of Clash Royale, but there's loads more to the game that you might be missing. Here's our rundown of some of the games' more interesting features that you might have missed in your rush to get fighting...

01

Card requests

If you're fed up of waiting for the Shop to offer cards you need, and the Chests aren't delivering them, then you can always ask your Clan members to donate to you. Simply swipe left to the Clan tab and request the card of your choice. Of course, if you're after something pretty rare, then be prepared for disappointment. But if you need something more common: a Musketeer or Archer, say, to complete your upgrade, it's the perfect way to get it!

02

Card donation

It works the other way too! Scrolling up and down the Clan Chat tab will show you requests from your fellow Clan members. Why would you donate? Well, apart from making your Clan stronger by helping your fellow teammate, you'll also be gifted some of that vital experience to increase your King Level and level up your Towers.

03 Player profile

If you've ever wondered just how much of your life you've sunk into Clash Royale (and you just might be terrified of the answer!), then you want the Player Profile page. You'll find it on the main screen right at the top. Tap the icon to the left of your player name to bring up the stats. You'll see how many wins you've had (including three Crown wins), as well as interesting factoids like the number of cards you've found, your current favourite card and more.

04 Training match

Although you can't win chests from training matches, they're a useful way of learning the ropes and testing out new cards. You'll be playing against the game, rather than a real person, but if you need to master new combos (eg how best to combine Hog Rider and Freeze spell for maximum devastation), then select your deck and go for it. The beauty of Training Matches is that even if you lose, you won't dump trophies, meaning you can mess around to your heart's content.

05 Achievements

Everyone loves winning gold stars, and you can rack 'em up in Clash Royale as well as school. In the game, you can get gold achievement stars for things as basic as joining a clan (the benefits are huge – do it!) and watching replays, to stretch goals like donating 250 cards to your team mates. The more stars you win, the more experience and gems you earn for doing so. You'll find your current Achievement goals by tapping on the rosette icon on the right hand side of the main page.

06 Activity log

One of the genius things about Clash Royale is that it records the games you play. So if you've snatched a famous, last-gasp victory that you want to relive; or if you've been outplayed comprehensively by an opponent and want to study their tactics, you can tap on the scroll icon on the main page to bring up a list of recorded recent games. As well as seeing the scoreline and your rival's deck, you can even share your replay for others to watch, as well as playing it back in slo-mo or ultra quick time.

07 Top Royales

Tapping on the Trophy icon on the main page opens the Top Royales leaderboard, which is a list of the best players, clans and friends that you can filter by global or local ranking. You can even delve into individual clans to check out player stats if you like. It's your individual trophy count that determines which Arena you're playing on, and therefore which cards you can find in chests, so it's all important stuff!

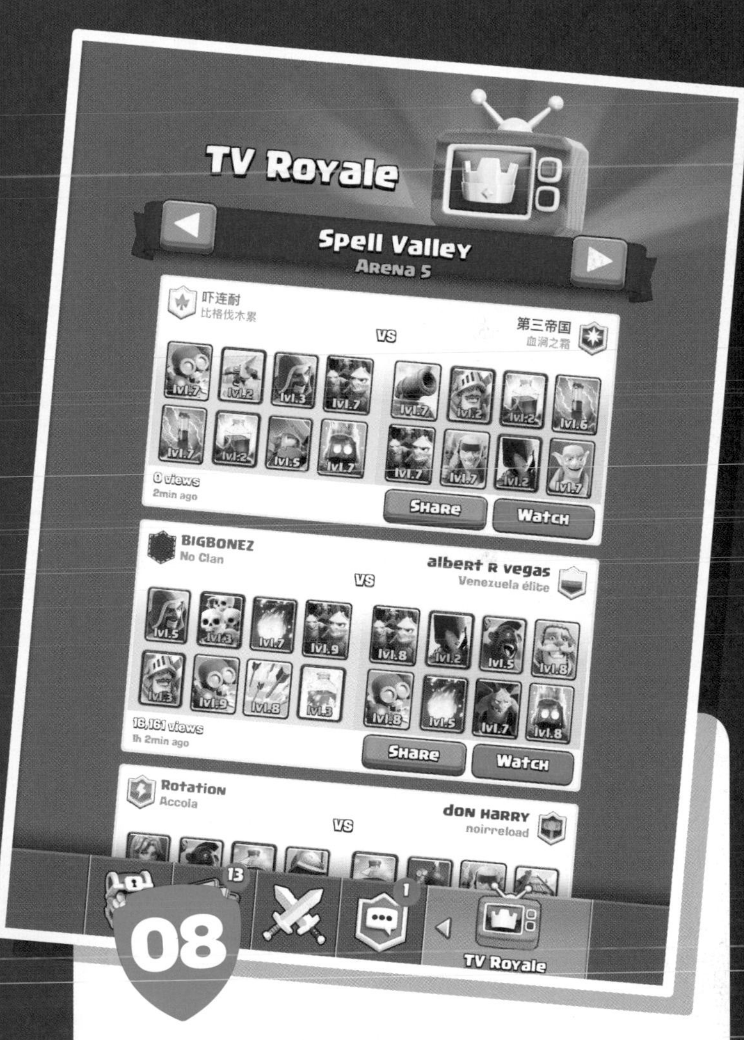

08 TV Royale

Who doesn't love watching tele when they're not playing games? Well you can watch some of the biggest and best games in TV Royale. Swipe left twice to open the set and you'll see some of the top Clash Royale gamers in action. Not only is it useful to study others' tactics, but you'll probably get to some some Epic cards in action that you don't yet own.

CLASH ROYALE STRATEGY GUIDE

There's almost no end to the different tactics you can use in Clash Royale. But here are some of our favourite tried-and-tested strategies for success.

Clash Royale is a game of tactics, wits, and deck-building that pits two players against one another in arena combat.

Your goal is simple: destroy the enemy's three crown towers while protecting you own. But you can use any number of strategies to complete this goal - flooding the board with weedy grunts, summoning powerful heroes with huge heath bars, or calling on strange magical powers to scorch your enemies.

Victory isn't just a matter of attack - it's a careful balancing act of offensive and defensive play.

So here are our tips and tricks to help you outwit, outmanoeuvre, and outplay your enemy.

01 Don't get flustered

Once your opponent starts dropping cards, it's easy to get carried away and just start throwing troops into the arena as fast as you can. You're better off staying calm and trying to counter each card that your enemy plays. So, if they drop a bunch of melee troops, play flying units to take them out from above. If they play a horde, unleash your Arrows to wipe them out.

02 Don't sit on 10 elixir

Elixir is the pink stuff that you spend to play cards, and it constantly regenerates as you play. You can't ever have more than 10 at any time though, so it's very important that you keep an eye on your elixir bar at the bottom of the screen. Once it's completely full, you'll have to start playing cards, or else you'll be wasting this precious resource.

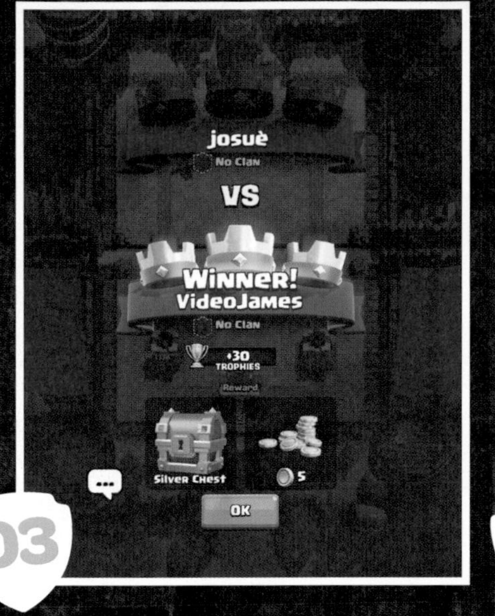

03

Use your crown towers

Destroying crown towers is the only path to victory in Clash Royale. But remember that you have an archer at the top of each of your crown towers, and this little bowman will fire arrows on any enemy troops that get near. You can use low-cost units to delay the enemy armies keeping them in the firing line.

04

Build a balanced deck

It can be tempting to fill your battle deck with high-cost cards and exotic spells, but you won't win many battles that way. Instead, you should try to ensure your deck contains a mixture of cheap melee troops, flying units, and higher-cost heroes. It's important to include a situational spell or two as well - perhaps Fireball or Arrows.

05

Keep an eye on the enemy

It's worth keeping on eye on the cards your enemy plays and think about their elixir level too. You might notice that they don't have many ranged troops. Then you can send out plenty of air units to exploit that weakness. If they've spent a lot of elixir on the left side of the arena, it could be a perfect time to counterattack on the right.

06

Play for elixir advantage

The surest path to consistent victories in Clash Royale is to build up and maintain an elixir advantage over your opponent. Basically, if you find yourself heading into the final phase of a battle and you have nine elixir, you're almost certain to beat an enemy who has just two or three. Managing elixir is key to victory.

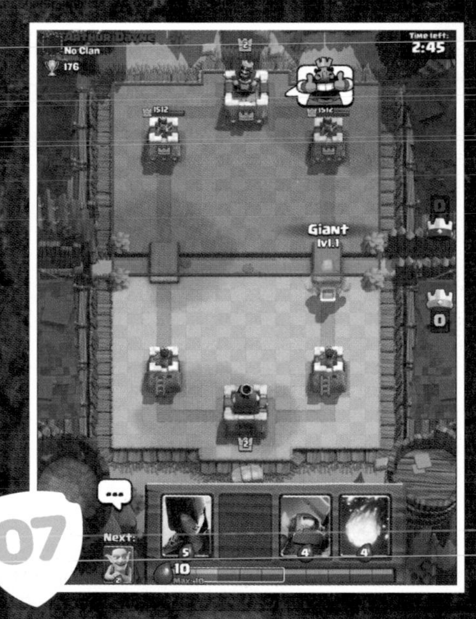

07

Trade low-cost for high

The best way to gain an elixir advantage over your opponent is to use low-cost cards to destroy the enemy's high-cost cards. So, if your enemy plays a Minion Horde for five elixir, and you wipe it out by playing the Arrows spell for just three elixir, you've gained a two elixir advantage. Consistently do this to win!

08

Remember defender advantage

Defenders usually have an advantage in Clash Royale because of the damage crown towers deal to enemy troops. Similarly, at the very start of a match it's usually (not always though!) advantageous to play second. That way, you can see what your opponent plays and put down something cheap to counter it.

09

Learn the damage types

Different troops deal damage in different ways. For instance, the Mini P.E.K.K.A can only attack at close range and only target one enemy at a time. Therefore, if you swarm him with skeletons or attack him from range, you'll have the upper hand. The Valkyrie, meanwhile, will crush an army of Skeletons.

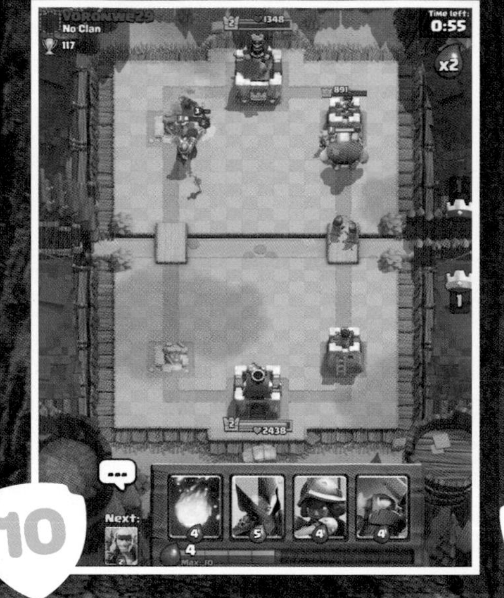

10

Take advantage of tanks

Troops with lots and lots of health are often referred to as 'tanks', and you'll want to make use of these tough customers to defend your weaker units. The Musketeer, for example, can deal a lot of damage, but doesn't have a lot of health. Partner her up with a Giant to take all the damage while the Musketeer provides support.

11

Learn to quick-drop

When you start playing Clash Royale, you'll probably use a single finger to drag a card from the bottom of the screen. That's fine and dandy, of course, but try tapping the card you want to play and then using your other hand to tap the arena square you wish to summon it onto. It'll appear right away, and you'll be able to play another card immediately.

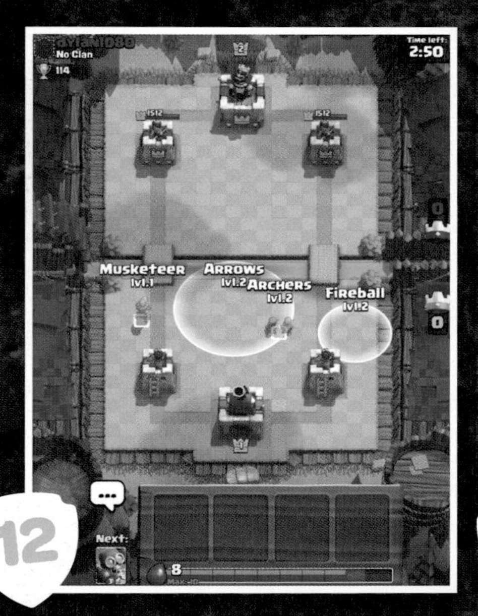

12

And maybe try the multi-drop

If you want to play two cards at the exact same time, you can make use of the multi-drop. Simply use two fingers to drag and drop two cards simultaneously, and they'll pop into life on the board side-by-side. You can even use four fingers to drag all four cards onto the board at once, assuming you have enough elixir.

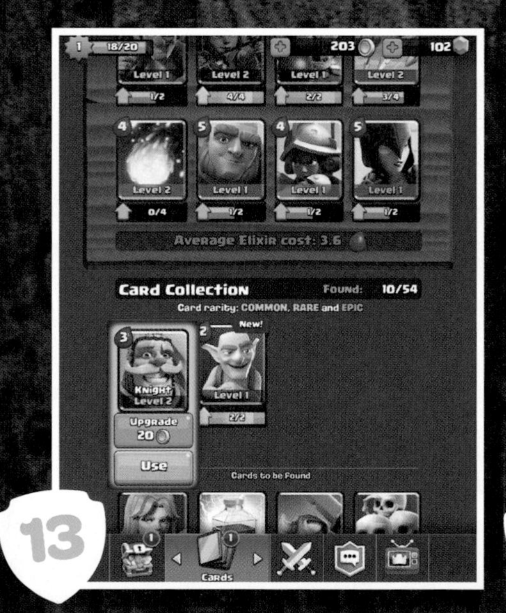

13

Don't upgrade all your cards

Gold coins are a precious commodity in the Clash Royale world, earned from chests. As such, you should be careful not to spend too much too quickly, and a good way to minimise your expense is to only level-up the cards you currently use in your battle deck. Also worth keeping an eye on the shopkeeper's wares each day.

14

Shuffle your hand

Ever found yourself in the middle of a battle only to discover that your entire hand is filled with expensive cards that aren't useful to your current situation? If so, you'll want to consider placing more low-cost cards in your deck. Not only are they often useful for gaining elixir advantage, but low-cost cards also let you shuffle your hand, freeing up space.

15 Distract enemy troops

When a tough troop crosses the bridge onto your side of the arena, it's often worth playing a low-cost unit like Goblins or Skeletons near the centre of the field to distract it. Timed correctly, your troops will cause the enemy to change course, taking damage from both your soldiers and your crown tower's archer.

16 Push to victory

Giants and P.E.K.K.A.'s look heavy, but these slow-moving units can actually be pushed by your smaller, quicker troops. Simply deploy your pusher directly in front of your crown tower, and then drop your tank below the arena bridge. The pusher should arrive just as your tank spawns, and boost its move speed across the map. It's a small but important difference.

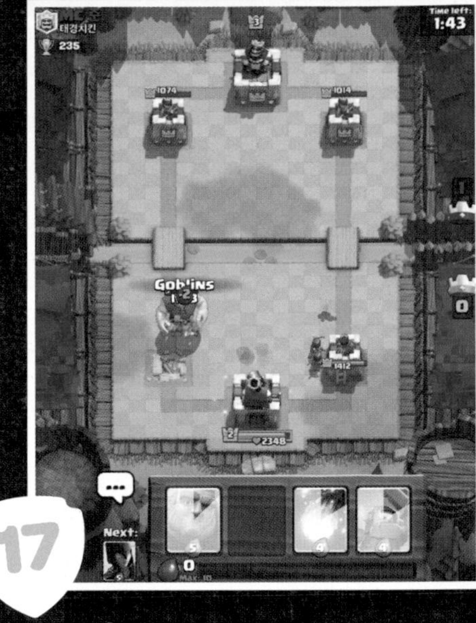

17 We have you surrounded

Skeletons, Goblins, and Barbarians are all powerful, but they share a weakness to splash damage. However, if there's a Witch or Wizard running towards your crown tower, try dropping a squad of Skeletons directly on top of the hostile spellcaster. Timing is crucial, but get it right and you can take them out.

18 Lure stronger foes

Distracting your foes is handy, and this technique is basically a chain of distraction. You can bait enemy units further and further across the map by placing one low-cost troop card after another just out of their reach. Once mastered, you can turn enemy troops around and run them back onto the other side of the arena, ensuring they get constantly hit by your towers.

19 Figure out the Elixir Collector

Given that you're playing for elixir advantage, a card that generates elixir has the potential to win matches. The Elixir Collector costs five elixir to play but generates seven units for you. Played effectively, it can provide just the edge you need to win those close matches, or it can bait out enemy spells like Fireballs.

20 Gamble!

If you can guess which card your enemy is about to play, you can get a crucial advantage. For example, once your Giant gets anywhere near the enemy tower, there's a good chance they might be about to play a swarming unit like Skeleton Army to attack it. So, if you like a gamble, you can send in a swarm of Arrows or a Fireball just beforehand.

CLASH ROYALE CARD GUIDE!

Whatever your strategy, the chances are that troop cards will form the backbone of your deck, but knowing which combinations of cards work best together can take a lot of practice and experimentation. So we've saved you the hassle, explaining all 33 of Clash Royale's troops with expert advice, tricks, and tips. To war!

Archers

These stylish sharpshooters may be slow, but they're also cheap to play and capable of outputting decent damage when supporting other allies. You might use them to protect a Giant as he advances towards enemy lines, for instance, or place them at the back of the field to defend your crown towers.

Baby Dragon

This little lizard is a versatile flying unit with plenty of health and he's capable of spitting scorching fireballs at his enemies. Although his fiery breath doesn't do a huge amount of damage to crown towers, he's excellent against enemy troops, especially swarms of low-level foes such as Goblins and Skeletons.

Balloon

This deadly flying unit deals massive damage to buildings using bombs, and can only be harmed by ranged enemies, making it a potentially game-winning card. Support it with a Baby Dragon that can target hostile Archers and Musketeers, or use the Freeze spell to encase your foe's defences in a layer of ice.

Barbarians

A group of four moustachioed melee fighters that can cut down crown towers in a few seconds flat if left unchecked. Barbarians are especially effective if they're supported with ranged troops like Archers or Musketeers, but remember that they're very vulnerable to enemy spells.

Bomber

This spindly skeleton may be weak, but it can deal a lot of damage in the right circumstances. Paired with a beefy buddy such as a Giant or Mini P.E.K.K.A., the Bomber can fling his explosives at enemy hordes or crown towers while its larger allies protect it from damage.

Dark Prince

This villainous mounted unit deals damage across an area, making him extremely effective against hordes of weaker foes. And once he gathers speed on his nimble steed, he'll unleash a charge attack that deals double damage, too. Pair him with the Prince for a destructive duo.

Fire Spirits

A fast-moving kamikaze unit that's best used to counter enemy attacks. Their area-of-effect damage means that Fire Spirits are handy for taking out large groups of foes such as Skeletons, Goblins, or even Barbarians. They're less useful against crown towers, however, so it's wise to save them for defensive plays.

Giant

A unit that only attacks buildings may sound a little weak, but this lumbering beast is one tough customer. His hefty healthbar means the Giant can be used to protect weaker troops such as the Bomber or Archers, soaking up damage while your allies toss out projectiles.

Giant Skeleton

This towering bag of bones isn't just a tough melee fighter - he also carries an enormous explosive that detonates when he dies. So, even if your opponent manages to gather enough troops to take out this monster, there's every chance they'll be blown to smithereens shortly after.

Goblins

These low-cost greenskins might not be glamorous, but they can actually deal a lot of damage, especially if they're shielded from harm by a big friendly unit. They're also a great way to distract higher-cost enemy troops, slowing your foe down while your crown towers pelt them.

Golem

This stony beast is slow, expensive, and one of the toughest troops in the entire game. It's best to place the Golem behind your crown towers so that you can support its advance with ranged troops such as Musketeers. And, when the enemy finally cuts down this monster, it explodes into two smaller Golemites.

Guards

If you like Skeletons but find that they're a little fragile, Guards are the answer. These melee troops carry great big wooden shields to deflect damage, allowing them to absorb attacks from even the most aggressive of foes. Use them to take down high-damage enemies.

Hog Rider

A powerful offensive card that's fast-moving, tough, and deals a heck of a lot of damage to buildings. He can even jump the river in the centre of the arena to reach its targets super-quick. Pair it with the Freeze spell to bypass enemy troops and cut down a crown tower in no time.

Ice Wizard

This cool customer makes use of powerful magic that not only deals damage but can also slow enemy movement and attack speed. He's handy for slowing foes in front of your crown towers, or you could pair him with a Giant and use his powers to keep the big chap alive for longer.

Knight

This handsome fellow has fairly high damage and health for a fairly low elixir cost, making him an ideal shield for weaker allies or a solid offensive option when supported with other troops. As a melee fighter he's super vulnerable to air units, though, so watch out for enemy Minions and Baby Dragons.

Miner

The humble shovel may not sound too scary, but this grubby chap uses his trusty spade to tunnel across the arena. As such, he's the perfect pick for surprise attacks, since you can deploy him anywhere on the board. He's great at dismantling Elixir Collectors.

Lava Hound

As if a huge healthbar wasn't scary enough, this flying beast will split into six Lava Pups upon death, forcing your enemy to commit an awful lot of resources to the fight. Despite its massive reserve of hitpoints, though, the Lava Hound actually does very little damage .

Mini P.E.K.K.A

This brutish battlebot has an awful lot of strength but just a handful of hitpoints, making it especially vulnerable to swarms of weedy foes such as Skeletons and Goblins. To get around this you should deploy a Giant, which will soak up hits while your little robot pal deals some serious damage.

Minion Horde

A swarm of six winged monsters that can make short work of any ground-based melee fighters. The Minion Horde is an excellent support for Giants and other big units, able to take out Goblins and Skeletons as your allies advance. Watch out for the Arrows spell though.

Minions

This trio of flying beasties will usually get shot down pretty quickly by your enemy's crown towers, so they're best saved for defensive purposes. They're super useful for dealing with dangerous enemy air units such as the Balloon, though, and they can pick off melee troops without taking any damage.

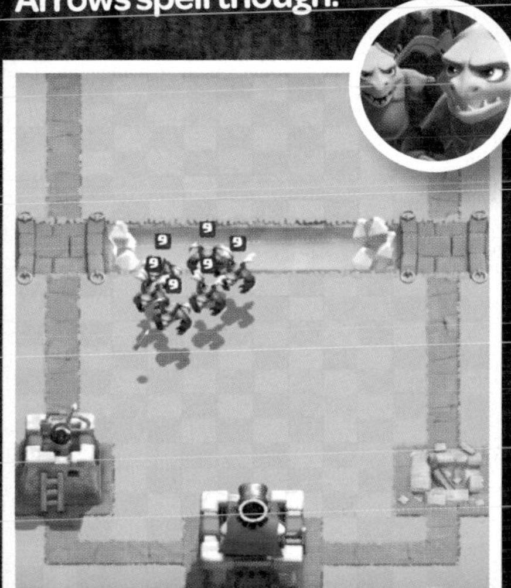

Musketeer

This long-range gunner can deal considerable damage from afar, but is a little on the squishy side when it comes to health. She's great at supporting Giants as they advance up the arena, and she can even destroy enemy cannons from a distance - shelling them to bits without taking a single hit!

P.E.K.K.A.

A colossal mechanical unit with a huge reserve of hitpoints, the P.E.K.K.A. is capable of ripping enemy crown towers to pieces if left unattended. Unfortunately, it's easily distracted by opposition troops and buildings, so you'll have to place this monster carefully.

Prince

This regal fellow may not be the toughest troop in your army, but once he picks up speed he can unleash a powerful charge attack for double damage. The Prince can only target one enemy at a time, though, making him vulnerable to swarms of foes. Pair him with the Witch or Dark Prince for best results. Use Skeletons against him.

Princess

Long-range and low-cost. Because her arrows deal area-of-effect damage, the Princess can make short work of enemy hordes, tearing through Goblins and Skeletons from a distance. Deploy her at the bottom of the arena to defend your towers.

Skeleton Army

A card that summons a shambling horde of 20 bony buddies - perfect for taking down tough enemies that can only target one opponent at a time. They'll wipe out a Giant, Prince, or P.E.K.K.A. in mere moments, but remember that they're super weak to Arrows, Baby Dragons, Wizards, Witches and Valkyrie.

Royal Giant

Rather than bashing buildings to bits with his fists, this hulking hero uses an enormous cannon to target enemy buildings. Pair him with a Princess and the two will bombard your opponent from a distance while the Royal Giant soaks up enemy damage.

Skeletons

This four-person squad of skeletal warriors costs just one elixir, making it the cheapest card in the game. This makes Skeletons especially handy for distracting more powerful units on their way to your buildings - they might not survive the encounter, but they'll give your tower archers a few precious extra seconds.

Sparky

A reinforced tank that deals tremendous damage from a gigantic lightning gun. But while Sparky may be powerful, she's also slow in terms of movement and attack speed. As such, it's a good idea to deploy Sparky alongside a Bomber or Princess.

Spear Goblins

This trio of ranged attackers is cheap to play and handy in a variety of situations, making the card an excellent addition to any deck. They can support tougher enemies such as Giants as you advance on enemy towers, face off against weaker air units, or defend your own towers.

Three Musketeers

A powerful trio of long-range gunners, but also the single most expensive card in the game, costing a whopping nine elixir to play. Given their high cost, it's wise to deploy the Three Musketeers at the bottom of the arena, giving your elixir time to recharge.

Witch

A supernatural summoner, the Witch uses magical projectiles to deal explosive damage. This makes the Witch strong against swarms of enemies, sure, but it's her ability to automatically summon three skeletons every few seconds that makes this spellslinger really worthwhile.

Valkyrie

This warrior woman carries an enormous axe which she swings in a circle, dealing damage in all directions. As such, she can reduce a Skeleton Army to a pile of bones in no time. Partner her with a Mini P.E.K.K.A. and the two can bash aside almost any opposition.

Wizard

Much like the Witch, this hooded spellcaster throws magical fireballs to deal area-of-effect damage. His spells are a little more powerful than the Witch's, though, making him useful for picking off enemy swarms whether they travel by air or ground. Minions, Goblins, Skeletons, and even Barbarians are all at risk from his powerful magic.

CLASH ROYALE BUILDINGS GUIDE!

Knights might have great moustaches and Fireballs may be flashy, but sometimes plain old bricks-and-mortar buildings are the key to victory. So, whether you're looking for a defensive structure to keep the enemy hordes at bay, or a powerful siege weapon to rain damage upon your opponent's towers from a distance, we can recommend just the card to help.

Barbarian Hut

It's expensive, but this sturdy structure will throw out two Barbarians every couple of seconds. Combine with troop cards to overwhelm your opponent.

Bomb Tower

A powerful defensive structure that will make short work of small to medium-size enemy ground troops. It's vulnerable against air attack, though, so watch out.

Cannon

A powerful defence against ground troops, but it's totally unable to target flying enemies. It's especially handy for drawing Giants away from your towers.

Elixir Collector

Although it costs five elixir to play, this magical powerplant will pay you seven elixir back - so long as your opponent doesn't destroy it first...

Furnace

A bubbling cauldron that spits out a pair of Fire Spirits every ten seconds, making it especially useful against decks with lots of Skeletons and Goblins.

Goblin Hut

These rustic little sheds will spawn a steady stream of Spear Goblins. It's usually best to place them behind your towers, safe from any marauding enemy soldiers.

Inferno Tower

This powerful tower inflicts huge damage on single targets, making it the ideal defence against Giants, Balloons, and Golems. Not so good against weaker swarms, though.

Mortar

This long-range bomb-lobber can target enemy towers from the other side of the arena, but it's vulnerable up close. Drop it and then defend it.

Tombstone

A spooky spawnpoint for Skeleton soldiers, and a great way to distract high-damage enemies like the Prince or P.E.K.K.A. who'd otherwise bash your towers to bits.

Tesla

This electrical apparatus lurks underground between charges, making it difficult for enemies to remove with fireballs or rockets. Effective against hordes of low-health troops.

X-Bow

This siege machine can target towers from the other end of the arena. Protect it well, and it can even take out your opponent's crown tower, winning you the match.

CLASH ROYALE BEST CARDS VS WORST CARDS!

Although every card in Clash Royale can be useful in the right situation, the very best are helpful in a wide variety of different circumstances. As such, it's often the humble low-cost cards that find their way into the top-tier decks, while expensive powerhouses sit on the sidelines. Here's our guide to three of the best and three of the worst cards for your arena battles.

THREE OF THE BEST

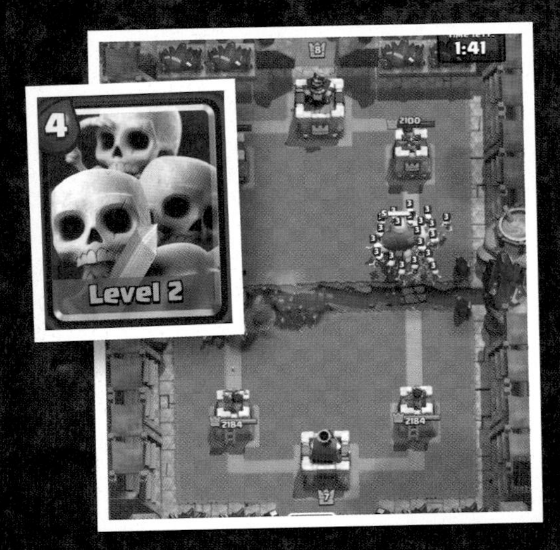

Hog rider

Quite possibly the strongest offensive card in the game, the Hog Rider is fast, tough, and can devastate enemy crown towers – especially if you manage to upgrade him a few levels. He can leap the river, meaning he can be played anywhere on the map too. Couple with a Freeze spell once he reaches a tower.

Skeleton army

These bundles of bone are supremely versatile. Their best use is to surround expensive enemies like Giants or P.E.K.K.A.'s which are approaching a vulnerable tower, however, the Skeleton Army can also be an effective offensive tower card, and can make mincemeat of enemy buildings. Just avoid arrows!

Zap

This spell may not do a whole lot of damage, but it's powerful enough to decimate hordes of weaker enemies. There's nothing more satisfying than Zapping an entire army of Skeletons, Minion Hordes and Goblins descending on your tower.

THREE OF THE WORST!

Three Musketeers

The single Musketeer is a great support card and the bane of Baby Dragons and Cannons. However, spending a whopping nine elixir on the Three Musketeers card is rarely a good idea. It completely wipes out your elixir reserves, and as a unit, they're still extremely vulnerable to Fireballs and splash damage.

Lava Hound

It can be tempting to add the toughest unit in the game to your deck, but it costs a massive seven elixir and does fairly little damage – even the Lava Pups it splits into are pretty weak. The Lava Hound's best use is to soak up damage for your weaker troops, allowing them slightly safer passage to the enemy towers.

Tesla

At first glance, this defensive structure seems great - dealing damage when enemies are near and then retreating underground when they're not, making it hard to target with fireballs. A Giant or similar unit will make light work of it though, and Cannons, Bomb Towers, and Inferno Towers are better in almost all situations.

CLASH ROYALE SPELLS GUIDE!

Sometimes there's just no substitute for a supernatural fireball or a freakishly large rocket. At times like these, you'll want to throw down one of Clash Royale's spell cards. There's ten to choose from, so whatever kind of deck you're creating you can be sure there's a magical power that'll slot right in.

Arrows

Unleash a hail of arrows upon your foe! This spell's perfect for clearing large groups of low-health enemies such as Skeletons, Goblins, or Minions.

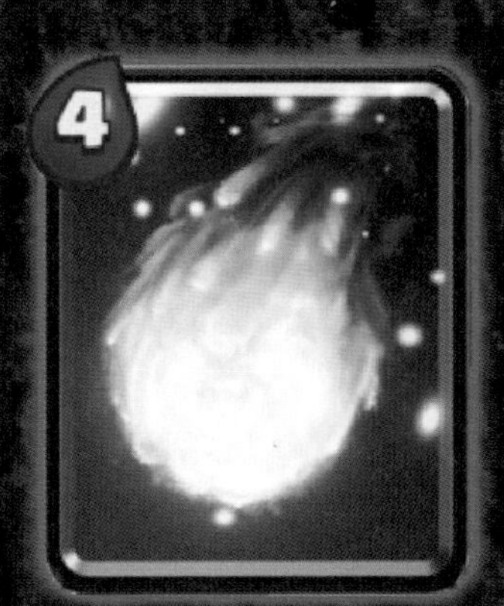

Fireball

A versatile blast of fiery damage. It's handy for scorching groups of smaller enemies, singeing tougher single units, or chipping away at your opponent's towers.

Freeze

This icy ability prevents any targets from attacking for a precious few seconds, and it's effective against buildings, troops, and even enemy towers.

Goblin Barrel

This card lets you fling a batch of daredevil Goblins deep into enemy territory. Wait until the coast is clear, then chuck it at your foe's tower for hefty damage.

Lightning
This card's okay against troops, but it deals major damage to structures of all types - perfect for those moments when your foe's filling the board with buildings.

Mirror
This nifty spell lets you play the same card twice in a row, although you'll have to pay one more elixir than usual for the privilege. Two Giants you say? No problem...

Poison
When your opponent starts filling the arena with low-cost troops, Poison is the perfect answer, slowing down enemies and dealing damage across a huge area.

Rage
A supercharged spell that speeds up all of your troops so that they'll dash across the arena licketysplit. Wait for an opening, then rush to victory!

Rocket
This explosive card deals more damage than any other spell in the game, making it the ideal weapon to take down your enemy's crown tower from afar.

Zap
A handy low-cost spell that stuns enemy troops for one second. It only affects a small area, though, so make sure you aim carefully.

CLASH ROYALE THE BEST CHESTS!

Some of the best rewards in Clash Royale come from treasure chests. Some are free, while others are so rare that you might need to use gems to buy 'em. Here's your guide to all the best chests, and the goodies inside...

Free Chest

You'll receive one of these freebie treasure troves automatically every four hours, and you can hold up to two of them at a time. Give them a tap and they unlock instantly, awarding a grab-bag of gems, coins, and cards. Like all chests, you'll receive more goodies at higher arena levels, but they generally contain lots of common cards.

Silver Chest

For every battle you win, you'll receive a Silver, Gold, Giant, Magical, or Super Magical Chest. You can hold up to four at any time and Silver is by far the most common of the bunch. It takes three hours to open and contains a small handful of gold and cards, although it's generally stuffed full of common cards.

Gold Chest

Gold Chests are rarer and more valuable than Silver ones, and they take eight hours to open. They always contain at least one rare card, although at higher arena levels they'll often hold two or more. They also award much greater quantities of gold than either Free or Silver Chests.

Giant Chest

Here's where things start getting good. The Giant Chest will occasionally drop as a reward for winning matches, or you can purchase it for 300 gems from the in-game shop. It takes 12 hours to open, but contains bloomin' loads of gold coins and at least eight rare cards. At higher arena levels, it can contain as many as 30 rares.

Crown Chest

For every 10 crowns you earn by destroying enemy towers, you'll receive a sparkling Crown Chest. Like the Free Chest, it opens instantly and contains a mix of gems, coins, and cards. It's more generous than the Free Chest, though, and it will always contain at least two rare cards.

Magical Chest

The Magical Chest costs 470 gems to buy, or if you're very, very patient, you can wait for one to drop as a post-game reward. These may contain fewer gold coins than the heaving Giant Chest, but each one is guaranteed to contain at least one epic card as well as several rares.

Super Magical Chest

The best of all the chests costs 2,500 gems to buy or will drop incredibly rarely as a reward for a victorious match. Naturally, it's bursting with goodies, including stacks of gold coins and at least 6 epic cards and 36 rares. At the very highest arena level, it awards 22 epics and 136 guaranteed rares.

THE GIANT QUIZ!

How much do you *really* know about your favourite games?

Are you a Giant genius? A Wizard whiz kid? Or do you have all the brains of a Barbarian? Sure, you probably know most of the troop names, and have a few spell strategies up your sleeves. But if you consider yourself a true mastermind, take our quiz and prove it!

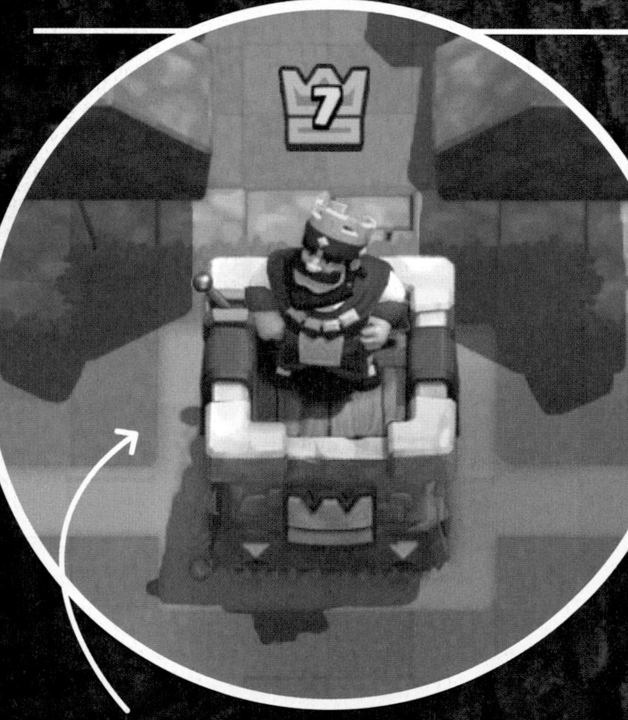

02 **Which of these will a Giant always attack first?**
A) Goblins
B) Buildings
C) Barbarians

03 **What is the Warrioris weapon in Boom Beach?**
A) Crystal Hammer
B) Diamond Mace
C) Ruby Sword

01 **What does the King Tower fire in Clash Royale?**
A) A cannon B) Fire C) Arrows

THE GIANT QUIZ!

04 Which of these is NOT a real spell in Clash of Clans?
A) Lightning
B) Earthquake
C) Avalanche

05 What airborne weapon features in Clash Royale?
A) Drone
B) Plane
C) Hot Air Balloon

06 How does the Valkyrie attack?
A) Spins her war axe B) Swings her sword C) Casts Viking spells

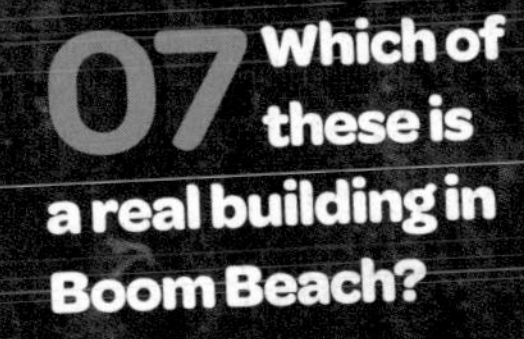

07 Which of these is a real building in Boom Beach?
A) Office
B) School
C) Quarry

08 Which of these is a real kind of Trap in Clash of Clans?
A) Summer B) Spring C) Winter

09 What are Power Stones used to make in Boom Beach? A) Statues
B) Houses C) Traps

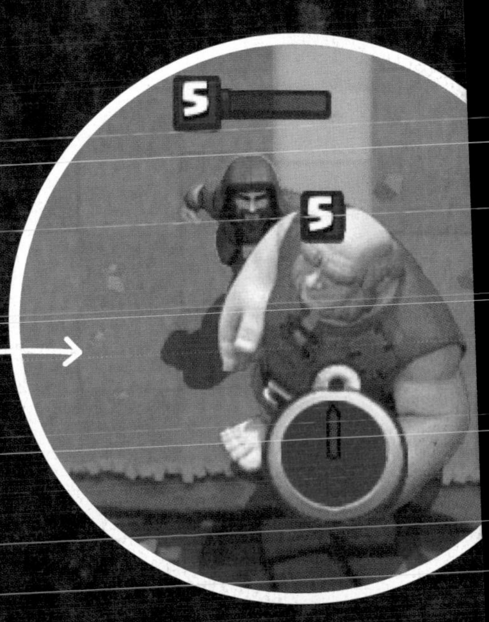

10 What do Wizards shoot? A) Fireballs
B) Snowballs
C) Meatballs

11 Who makes Clash of Clans, Boom Beach and Clash Royale? A) Cellshaded B) Supercell C) Supersonic

Place the Cannon in the center of the village. We must protect the Town Hall!

12 What does P.E.K.K.A stand for, after coming top of a Facebook contest? A) Perfect Enraged Knight Killer of Assassins B) Pretty English Knight Killer Army C) Proud Endangered Knight Killer Arsenal

13 How many cards do you choose for your whole deck in Clash Royale A) 20 B) 8 C) 18

14 What colour are the gems in Clash Royale? A) Yellow B) Red C) Green

15 What is Hog Rider's weapon? A) Dagger B) Pistol C) Hammer

16 What colour is Elixir in Clash Royale? A) Pink B) Blue C) Black

17 How many goblins leap out of a Goblin Barrel in Clash Royale? A) 5 B) 3 C) 2

18 When was the iPhone edition of Clash of Clans released? A) 2012 B) 2015 C) 2009

19 What does the Lava Hound split into when it dies? A) Lava Pups B) Fire Cats C) Flame Fish

20 In Clash Royale, the Witch can summon skeletons: how many appear with each spell she casts? A) 1 B) 2 C) 3

ANSWERS!

01: A
02: B
03: A
04: C
05: C
06: A
07: C
08: B
09: A
10: A
11: B
12: A
13: B
14: C
15: C
16: A
17: B
18: A
19: A
20: C

How did you do?

0-5: Skeleton: You don't know a lot about these games do you? Must try harder!

6-10: Prince: You've got plenty still to learn. Go play more!

11-15: Knight: Nice try. You may not be the main man, but you're nearly there!

16-20: King: You know these games inside out – well done!

MISSING PIECES!

Help fill the holes in this battle scene from Boom Beach!

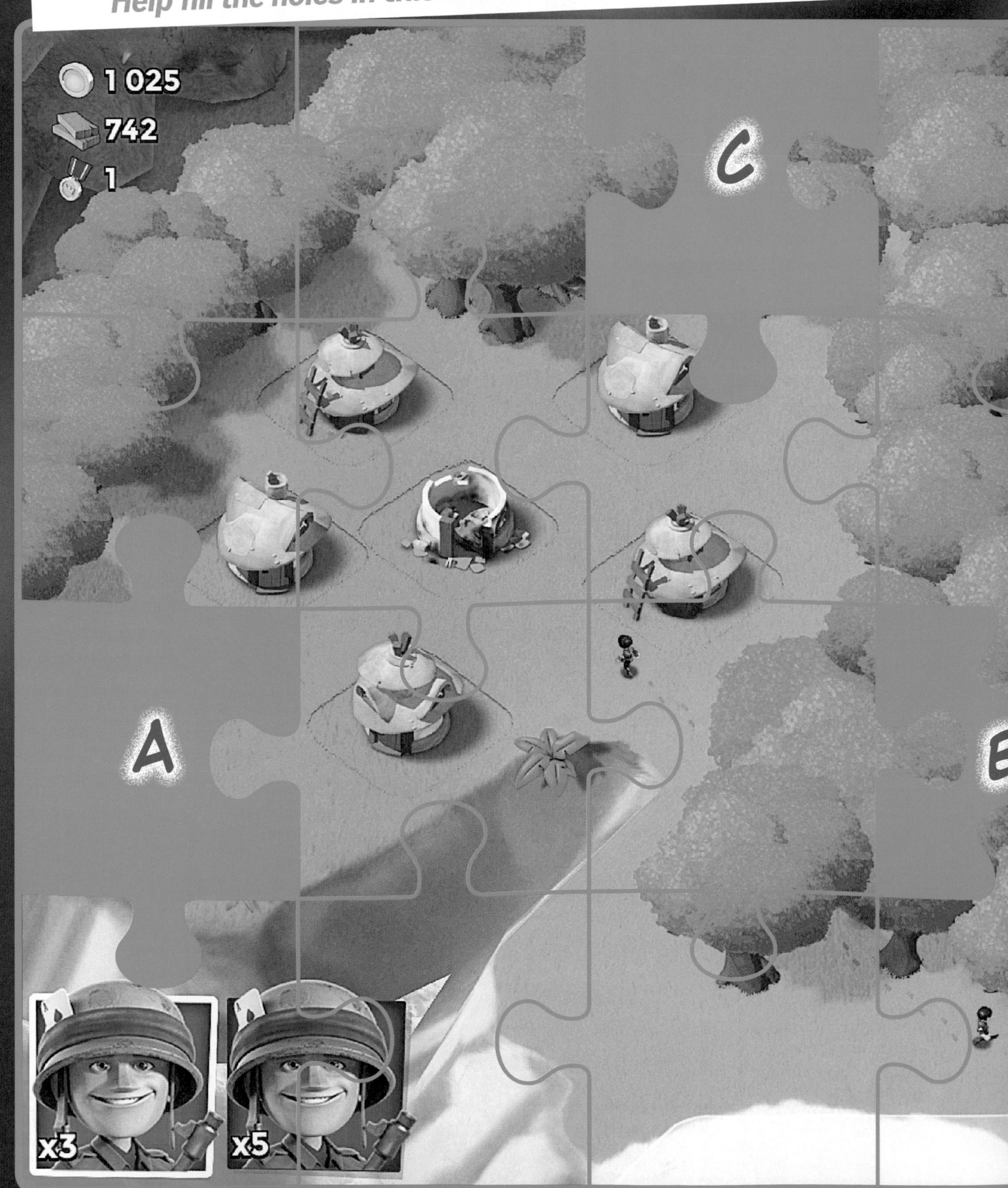

IT'S WAR! Or it will be once all the holes are filled in! Match the missing pieces of this Boom Beach island to the holes, and then check you're right - the answers are at the bottom of the page.

ANSWERS: A:4 B:2 C:1 D:3

WORDSEARCH

A	M	O	O	B	U	L	I	V	E
G	U	N	B	O	A	T	O	S	R
V	F	N	T	M	M	X	U	K	O
M	C	H	T	B	L	T	R	N	N
I	I	C	R	I	S	T	W	A	F
N	A	A	O	K	K	I	G	T	I
E	M	E	O	T	P	D	N	P	S
Q	S	B	P	S	J	S	E	L	T
A	D	O	S	H	S	F	U	M	Y
G	H	E	A	V	Y	O	T	K	S

Find the following words in the grid

BOOM
TANK
BOMB
MEDKIT
TROOPS
HEAVY
MINE
EVIL
GUNBOAT
BEACH

Answers:

A	M	O	O	B	U	L	I	V	E
G	U	N	B	O	A	T	O	S	R
V	F	N	T	M	M	X	U	K	O
M	C	H	T	B	L	T	R	N	N
I	I	C	R	I	S	T	W	A	F
N	A	A	O	K	K	I	G	T	I
E	M	E	O	T	P	D	N	P	S
Q	S	B	P	S	J	S	E	L	T
A	D	O	S	H	S	F	U	M	Y
G	H	E	A	V	Y	O	T	K	S

HOW TO DRAW THE BLUE KING!

Render this regal Royale by using our grid to guide you!

JUST COPY THE PATTERN, GOING SQUARE BY SQUARE. EASY!

YOU'LL have made a picture fit for a King, if you take your time. Use this template to guide you. Just follow the pattern above, making sure you focus on what's in each square. Use a pencil first, then finish your master-piece with pens!

SPOT THE DIFFERENCE...

Can you spot the 10 differences in these very similar scenes?

AT first glance, they look almost identical scenes, but look closer and you'll start to see some subtle differences. There are actually 10 differences between the two, but some are fiendishly different. See how many you can spot and write your answer in the space below...

HOW TO DRAW A BARBARIAN!

Master the Barbarian by using our simple grid to guide you!

JUST COPY THE PATTERN, GOING SQUARE BY SQUARE. SIMPLE!

WANT to draw the classic Barbarian? It's easy if you use our grid to guide you. Just follow the pattern above, making sure you focus on what's in each square. Try it in pencil first before going over your outline with pens!

WORDSEARCH

A	I	W	T	H	C	A	E	B	N
D	G	H	T	N	M	D	O	A	S
C	F	N	G	E	M	S	U	R	M
L	C	Z	K	L	L	N	R	B	A
A	I	W	O	I	S	A	W	A	G
S	A	I	P	X	L	L	G	R	I
H	M	Z	G	I	P	C	N	I	C
Q	S	A	O	R	J	S	M	A	I
A	D	R	A	H	G	I	A	N	T
M	E	D	I	C	O	A	T	K	T

Find the following words in the grid

BARBARIAN	GIANT
CLASH	MAGIC
MEDIC	ELIXIR
WIZARD	GEMS
BEACH	CLANS

Answers:

A	I	W	T	H	C	A	E	B	N
D	G	H	T	N	M	D	O	A	S
C	F	N	G	E	M	S	U	R	M
L	C	Z	K	L	L	N	R	B	A
A	I	W	O	I	S	A	W	A	G
S	A	I	P	X	L	L	G	R	I
H	M	Z	G	I	P	C	N	I	C
Q	S	A	O	R	J	S	M	A	I
A	D	R	A	H	G	I	A	N	T
M	E	D	I	C	O	A	T	K	T

Clash of Clans, Boom Beach and Clash Royale - in 26 letters!

A

Attack!

Who doesn't like a good battle? If there's one thing you know you're going to be doing a heck of a lot in any Supercell game, it's taking your troops out into the field. Whether charging into a rival township in Clash of Clans or storming the shore in Boom Beach, if you're not up for a fight, you're playing the wrong game.

B

Blackguard

If you need any motivation to take to the high seas in Boom Beach, the knowledge that out there are the Blackguard - the tyrannical force out to enslave your islanders the moment your back is turned - should do the trick. The fact they use a skull as a symbol, is the only hint you need that they're not

Clans

This one was kind of obvious, wasn't it? Clash of Clans would be nothing without its... well, clans. Attaching yourself to a faction not only allows you to donate troops to one another, but also opens up the world of clan warfare, allowing you to loot and destroy rival factions with the backing of your team. It pays to band together.

Defence

As much as you might like to go on the offensive, life in any of Supercell's games relies on balance, and that means building up your base in Clash of Clans and Boom Beach so that they aren't a walkover for invading forces eager to bash up your barbarians and ransack your resources. You better firm up that fortress!

Elixir

Whether light or dark, Elixir is your lifeblood in Clash of Clans. It's why you raid rival bases, and it's what helps fuel your empire. Gather enough and you can expand your army and bolster their barracks. Dark Elixir lets you purchase those oh so important hero troops. In Clash Royale, it's the currency you need to play your cards.

F

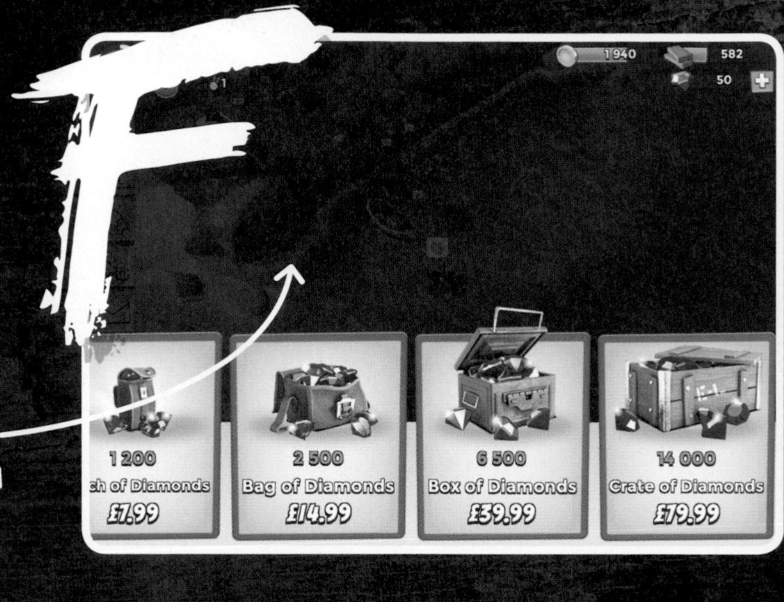

Free-To-Play

Who knew the day would come when the biggest games on mobile were given away for free? All of Supercell's line-up can be picked up without charge, but bear in mind you can spend dosh aplenty buying extra resources and speeding up those pesky upgrades.

G

Global

Never in the history of mobile, possibly video games full stop, have a few titles so dominated so many gamers' time. Clump Clash of Clans, Boom Beach and Clash Royale together and, chances are, scores of folk you know are playing one, if not all, of Supercell's line-up.

SUP
ERC
ELL

Helsinki

In the summer it barely gets dark and in the winter you're lucky if you see light, but the Finnish capital city, Helsinki, is not only home to Supercell, but also some of the biggest and most creative game developers in the world, with the likes of Rovio of Angry Birds fame and Quantum Break's Remedy just down the road in Espoo.

I

Islands

Islands, island, islands. Boom Beach is a world populated by islands, each one ripe for conquer. Exploring and making a move on other player's bases in the area is what play is all about, with the game's world rich with unique archipelagos serving as Boom Beach's signature. Just don't count on your neighbours being all too friendly.

Jam

Take three different game styles, smush them together in a jam, and what do you get? Clash Royale. Part card battler, part tower defence, part multiplayer online battle arena (or MOBA for those in the know), play revolves around destroying enemy towers in small stages by playing the right cards at the right time.

King of the Hill

It's almost four years since Supercell unleashed the all conquering Clash of Clans upon the world and, bar the odd intervention by a certain Candy Crush Saga, has sat on top of the AppStore's top grossing charts in the UK and US for the best part of that time. Oh, and Boom Beach and Clash Royale aren't far behind, either.

Landing

It might not be Normandy, but there's certainly something of Saving Private Ryan when it comes to storming the beaches in Boom Beach, with your big guns firing from your ships back out at sea. Like warfare, planning which buildings to target in which order before sending your troops in is key to victory.

M

Magic

Want to collect new cards or upgrade your existing pack in Clash Royale? Magic is the key - or, rather, magical chests. Winning battles unlocks these chests, with play ranking them from Silver, Golden and Giant chests at the bottom right through to Magical and Super Magical chests right up at the top.

N

Nautical

Fancy taking to the sea but worried that rolling and rocking motion of the ocean will cause you to spill your guts? Boom Beach's water world is the perfect way to experience island hopping from the safety of your mobile, with extra points on offer if you take it on while sat in the bath.

O

On The Box

Back in 2015, Supercell showed a fresh commercial during Super Bowl XLIX, with a one minute ad featuring megastar Liam Neeson reprising his role from the film Taken, in order to take revenge on an random player destroying his town in Clash of Clans. It was voted the second best Super Bowl ad that year!

AtoZ

P

Pals

What's the point in conquering the world if your friends can't see it? As you might expect, Clash of Clans, Boom Beach and Clash Royale all let you link up with your friends around the world, either via Facebook Connect or Game Center. You can even attack fellow clan members!

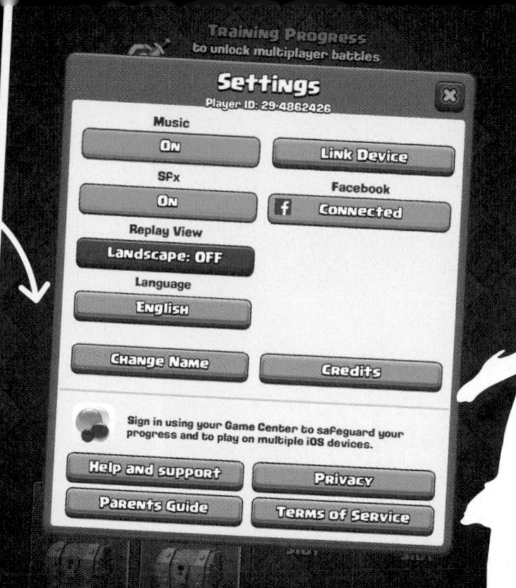

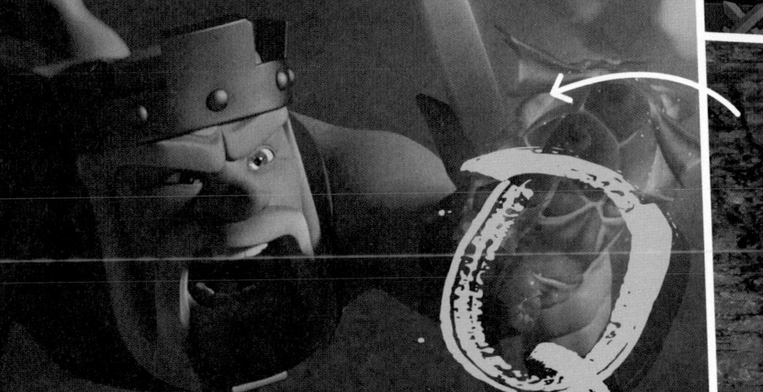

Quest

One thing that Clash of Clans and Boom Beach fans are calling out for are daily, weekly and monthly quests - so much so that many have taken to the games' official forums in order to draw out their own plans for how a such a system might work. As if we all need any more reasons to start them up?

Robes

Have you heard of Clash of Clans Cosplay? Yes, there are people attending games events all over the globe dressed in wizard costumes, either purchased off eBay or, if they're feeling particularly daring and cheap, made using their own dressing gowns from home. Either way, you know a game's made it when it inspires dress up time.

Social

More than 20 million people follow the official Clash of Clans Facebook page. That's a massive amount before you even tally the 2.2 million following Boom Beach, 658,000 following Clash Royale and the 666,000 following the official Supercell account. All in all, that's more than 23.5 million people!

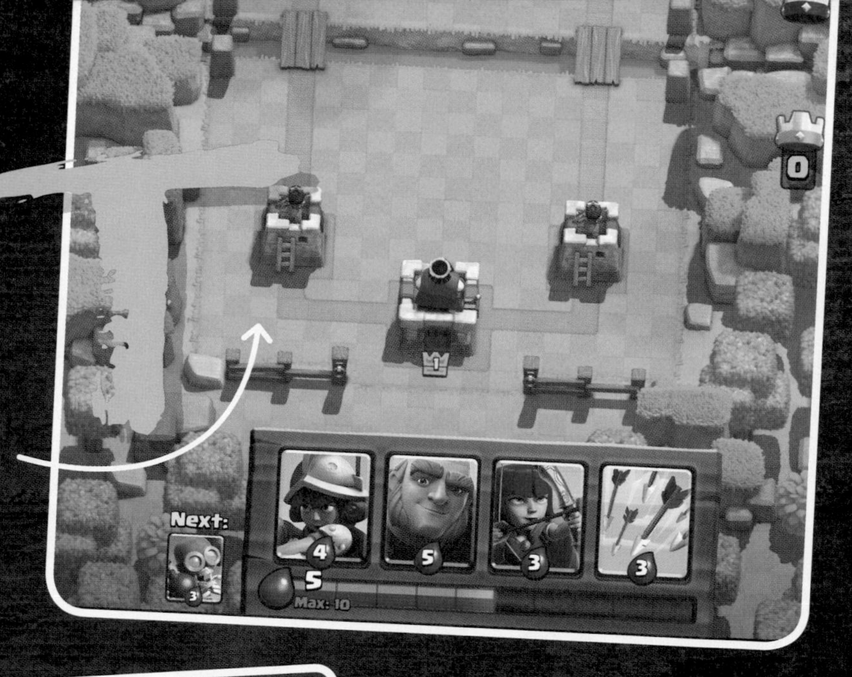

Towers

Whether you're taking on Clash Royale or its spiritual predecessor Clash of Clans, Towers are a big deal. In Clash Royale, each arena features three towers for each player, two sitting in the corners like tent pegs, and the King's Tower. Destroying them not only hands you crowns, but vital territory too.

Upgrade

Oh, the hours, days and weeks people spend waiting for buildings to upgrade in Clash of Clans and Boom Beach, but isn't that kind of the point? Good things come to those who wait, and the knowledge that each and every upgrade may take a stack load of time to complete makes it mean even more when it's done.

Victory

When it comes to battle, the only thing that matters is the victor. That's why all of Supercell's games give you the option to exact your revenge instantly, That's the cycle - the quest for victory means defeat doesn't dampen you down, it spurs you on for more!

Wheels

Back in June 2013, Supercell reportedly treated all of its employees to free bicycles as a kind of bonus, helping them to navigate their way through Helsinki's streets on the way to work and back. Sure, they might have preferred a Lamborghini each, but still a nice gift!

X-Men

Ever wanted to assemble your own band of superheroes? Success in Clash of Clans relies on you doing just that, mixing up barbarians with archers and goblins, giants with wizards and dragons. Focusing on one band of troops alone will never see you win the day.

Yarn

One of the great things about mobile MMOs like Clash of Clans and Boom Beach is that everyone plays out their own story. Everyone designs their own base, has their own skirmishes, joins their own clans and, in that kind of way, has their own unique experience.

Zzzzz

Sleep. You remember sleep, right? That was the thing you used to get before you joined a clan and decided to take on the world? That thing you'd head to bed for instead of landing on enemy beaches and taking down bases? No, neither do we, and we're not sure we miss it either!

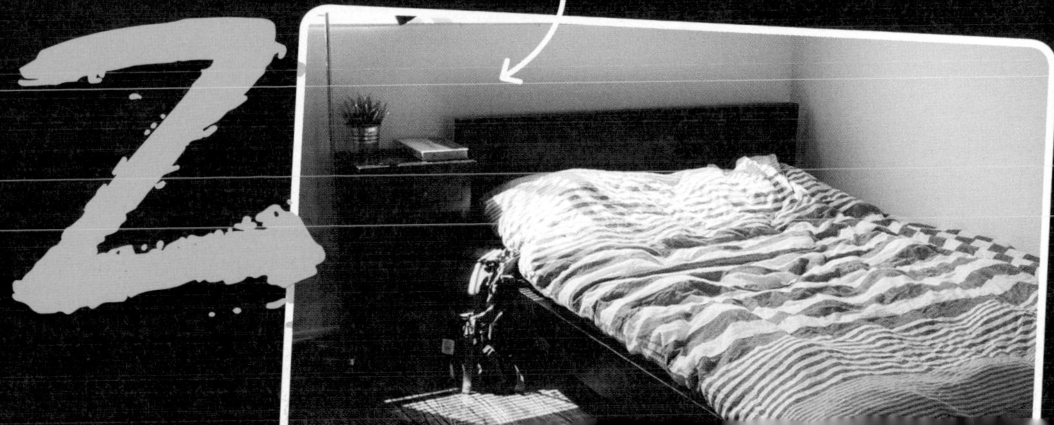